First World War
and Army of Occupation
War Diary
France, Belgium and Germany

59 DIVISION
176 Infantry Brigade
Prince of Wales's (North Staffordshire Regiment)
2/6th Battalion
1 January 1916 - 29 February 1916

WO95/3021/4

The Naval & Military Press Ltd
www.nmarchive.com
Published in association with The National Archives

Published by

The Naval & Military Press Ltd

Unit 10 Ridgewood Industrial Park,

Uckfield, East Sussex,

TN22 5QE England

Tel: +44 (0) 1825 749494

www.naval-military-press.com

www.nmarchive.com

This diary has been reprinted in facsimile from the original. Any imperfections are inevitably reproduced and the quality may fall short of modern type and cartographic standards.

© Crown Copyright
Images reproduced by permission of The National Archives, London, England, 2015.

Contents

Document type	Place/Title	Date From	Date To
Heading	WO95/3021/4		
Heading	War Diary of 2/6th Battalion North Stafford Regiment From 1st January 1916 To (Volume II)		
War Diary	St Albans	01/01/1916	29/01/1916
Heading	War Diary of 2/6th Battalion North Stafford Regt From February 1st 1916 To February 29th 1916 (Volume 2)		
War Diary	St Albans	01/02/1916	29/02/1916

w0095130214

17/59

(6)

Confidential.

WAR DIARY.

— of —

1/6th Battalion. North Stafford Regiment

From:- 1st January, 1916   to:-

(Volume II)

WAR DIARY
INTELLIGENCE SUMMARY

Army Form C. 2118.

(Volume 2)
Page 1

(Erase heading not required.)

Hour, Date, Place		Summary of Events and Information	Remarks and references to Appendices
1/1/16	ST ALBANS	Strength of Battalion this date:- Officers 24 Other ranks 606 Total Strength 630	Nat: all
2/1/16	DO	Battalion takes part in Divisional Administrative Scheme - Exercise on the work of Medical arrangements, Stretcher Bearers, and R.A.M.C. - Regimental Aid Posts being established for this purpose, and casualties dealt with	Nat: all
22/1/16	DO	Arrival of first draft of Army Reservists Class B men (60) from Administrative Centre (Derby Recruits)	Nat: all
24/1/16	DO	Battalion Messing now taken over by Messrs W. & H. Hyde, Government Contractors - Major J. H. Porter being the President of the Regimental Institute for this area	Nat: all
24/1/16	DO	100 Mo.C.E.III Rifles (new) with all accessories received	Nat: all
25/1/16	DO	Arrival of 20 Derby Recruits from Administrative Centre	Nat: all
26/1/16	DO	Arrival of 27 Derby Recruits from Administrative Centre	Nat: all
28/1/16 (3 A.M.)	DO	Inspection of Battalion Bombing &c at JACKSONS FIELD by The G.O.C. MAJOR-GENERAL R.N. READE. C.B.	Nat: all
29/1/16	DO	Arrival of 40 Derby Recruits from Administrative Centre	Nat: all

Commanding 2/- 6th Bn. N. Staff Reg^t.
Lt.-Col.

Confidential

War Diary

- of -

2/6th Battalion. North Stafford Regt.

from :- February 1st 1916.   to :- February 29th, 1916.

(Volume 2)

WAR DIARY
of
INTELLIGENCE SUMMARY
2/6th Battalion North Stafford Regt (Volume 2) Page 2

Army Form C. 2118.

Hour, Date, Place	Summary of Events and Information	Remarks and references to Appendices
1/2/16. ST ALBANS	Strength of Battalion this date:— Officers. Other Ranks. Total Strength 25. 773. 796. Halt	
2/2/16. Do	Arrival of 79 Recruits from Administrative Centre. Halt	
3/2/16. Do	First Court Martial in Bn't takes place, being a District Court Martial on No. 2683 PRIVATE T. GOULD, on a charge of using threatening language to a superior officer. Halt	
8/2/16. Do (11.30 a.m. NUNNERY FARM)	Inspection of the Derby Recruits by the G.O.C. (MAJOR-GEN. R.N. READE. C.B.) Halt	
11/2/16. ST ALBANS	Arrival of 46 Recruits from Administrative Centre. Halt	
14/2/16. Do	Arrival of 54 Recruits from Administrative Centre. Halt	
" Do.	MAJOR-GENERAL A.E. SANDBACH., C.B., D.S.O. takes over Command of the Division this date, vice MAJOR-GENERAL R.N. READE. C.B. Halt	
15/2/16. Do	General Muster Parade of Battalion (and throughout the Division) for the purpose of checking Rolls received from Territorial Force Records. The final check of Rolls for this Bn't to be made by Officers detailed for this purpose by 176th Brigade. Halt	

Halbul 2/ Lt-Col.
Commanding 6th Bn. N. Staff Regt.

WAR DIARY
INTELLIGENCE SUMMARY

26th Battalion (previously 20th) Stafford Regt (Volume 2) Page 3.

Army Form C. 2118.

Instructions regarding War Diaries and Intelligence Summaries are contained in F. S. Regs., Part II. and the Staff Manual respectively. Title pages will be prepared in manuscript.

Hour, Date, Place	Summary of Events and Information	Remarks and references to Appendices
16/2/16 ST. ALBANS	Colonel L. R. Carleton, D.S.O., G.S.O. takes over Command of 176th Infantry Brigade this date, vice Colonel L. H. Hall. Chandos Pole-Gell.	
" DO.	Arrival of 22 Recruits from Administrative Centre Half	
22/2/16 DO.	Third Army Letter 6890/1st Q. this date, instructs that War Establishments, Part VIII is now applicable to this Division. Half	
24/2/16 DO.	Instructions received from 176th Infantry Brigade for Week-end leave to be cancelled, and all officers and men away from Unit to be recalled. Half	
29/2/16 DO.	Orders received at 11 a.m. for Practice of an Emergency Move under Scheme B - the Battalion parading in two Columns at 3.30 p.m. and 7.15 p.m. respectively on the Markets Square. Orders then received for Parade to be dismissed. Men not to leave Billet area. Witnessed by Lieut-General Sir A. E. Codrington, K.C.V.O., Half C.B.	

H A Hill Lt.-Col.
Commanding 6th Bn. N. Staff Regt.

www.ingramcontent.com/pod-product-compliance
Lightning Source LLC
Chambersburg PA
CBHW081516160426
43193CB00014B/2702